Strategic User Experience Design

Optimizing Engagement: The Art of Strategic User Experience Design

writer name

DHAYANANDH RAVICHANDRAN

Table of Contents

WRITER'S NOTE

Hello, Dhayanandh Ravichandran here.

Welcome to "Strategic User Experience Design: Aligning User Needs with Business Goals." In today's rapidly evolving digital landscape, creating exceptional user experiences has become a paramount priority for organizations across industries. Gone are the days when UX design was merely about creating visually appealing interfaces or ensuring functionality.

Instead, it has evolved into a strategic discipline that requires a deep understanding of user behaviors, preferences, and motivations, coupled with a keen awareness of overarching business objectives.

This eBook serves as your comprehensive guide to navigating the complex terrain of strategic UX design. Whether you're a seasoned UX professional seeking to refine your approach or a newcomer eager to grasp the fundamentals, this resource is tailored to equip you with the knowledge and strategies needed to craft user experiences that deliver tangible value to your organization.

Throughout the following pages, we'll embark on a journey through the critical components of strategic UX design. We'll start by exploring the foundational importance of setting clear and measurable business goals, which serve as the North Star guiding our design decisions.

From there, we'll delve into the intricacies of user research and analysis, uncovering invaluable insights that will inform our design strategies and shape our user-centric approach.

But our exploration doesn't stop there. We'll also examine the significance of designing with the target audience in mind, understanding that every pixel, every interaction, and every decision we make must resonate with the needs and desires of our users. Moreover, we'll dive into the realm of measuring success metrics, recognizing that the efficacy of our design efforts must be quantifiable and actionable. And finally, we'll learn how to implement feedback loops, ensuring that our design iterations are iterative, responsive, and continuously optimized based on user insights.

By the time you reach the conclusion of this eBook, you'll have not only gained invaluable insights into the strategic principles of UX design but also developed a robust toolkit of strategies and techniques to drive business growth, foster customer loyalty, and differentiate your products or services in today's competitive marketplace. So, let's embark on this journey together and unlock the transformative power of strategic user experience design.

Chapter One
Understanding Strategic UX Design

> "
>
> Design: intellect made visible, innovation embodied in visual expression.

Strategic User Experience (UX) Design is more than just creating visually appealing interfaces or ensuring usability; it's about aligning design decisions with broader business objectives to drive success. Here, we'll delve into the fundamental principles and components of strategic UX design. Instead, it has evolved into a strategic discipline that requires a deep understanding of user behaviors, preferences, and motivations, coupled with a keen awareness of overarching business objectives.

At its core, strategic UX design involves integrating user needs, business goals, and market insights to create experiences that not only delight users but also deliver tangible value to the organization.

By strategically aligning UX efforts with business objectives, organizations can gain a competitive edge, enhance customer satisfaction, and drive growth.

Key Components of Strategic UX Design

1. User-Centric Approach

Strategic UX design begins with a deep understanding of the target audience's needs, preferences, and behaviors. By conducting thorough user research and creating detailed user personas, designers can empathize with users and tailor experiences that resonate with them.

2. Business Objectives Alignment

Successful UX design goes beyond addressing user pain points; it also supports overarching business goals. Design decisions should be guided by a clear understanding of the organization's objectives, whether it's increasing revenue, improving customer retention, or expanding market share.

3. Iterative Design Process

Strategic UX design is iterative in nature, allowing for continuous refinement and improvement based on user feedback and evolving business needs. By adopting an agile approach to design, teams can quickly test hypotheses, gather insights, and adapt their strategies accordingly.

4. Cross-Functional Collaboration

Collaboration between UX designers, product managers, developers, and other stakeholders is essential for aligning UX efforts with business goals. By fostering open communication and cross-functional collaboration, teams can ensure that design decisions are informed by a holistic understanding of user needs and business requirements.

5. Measurable Outcomes

Strategic UX design is results-oriented, with a focus on measuring the impact of design initiatives on key performance indicators (KPIs). By establishing clear success metrics and tracking performance over time, organizations can quantify the value of UX design and make data-driven decisions.

Strategic UX design is about more than just creating visually appealing interfaces; it's about driving business success through user-centered design practices. By integrating user needs with business objectives, adopting an iterative approach, fostering collaboration, and measuring outcomes, organizations can leverage the power of strategic UX design to create experiences that resonate with users and deliver measurable results.

CHAPTER TWO
Setting Business Goals

> ❝
>
> UX design is about creating a journey that delights users.

In strategic user experience (UX) design, setting clear and measurable business goals is paramount to ensuring that design efforts align with broader organizational objectives. Here, we'll explore the importance of establishing business goals and how they inform UX design decisions.

1. Guiding Design Direction

Business goals serve as a roadmap for UX design initiatives, providing clarity on what the organization aims to achieve. By aligning design efforts with these goals, UX professionals can prioritize features, functionalities, and design elements that directly contribute to business success.

2. Measuring Success

Clear business goals enable organizations to measure the impact of UX design on key performance indicators (KPIs) such as conversion rates, user engagement, and revenue generation. By defining success metrics upfront, teams can assess the effectiveness of their design strategies and make data-driven decisions.

3. Allocating Resources

Setting business goals helps allocate resources effectively, ensuring that UX design efforts are focused on initiatives that deliver the most significant value to the organization. By understanding the priorities and objectives of the business, UX professionals can allocate time, budget, and talent accordingly.

How to Set Business Goals for UX Design:

1. Understand Organizational Objectives

Business goals serve as a roadmap for UX design initiatives, providing clarity on what the organization aims to achieve. By aligning design efforts with these goals, UX professionals can prioritize features, functionalities, and design elements that directly contribute to business success.

2. Define Key Performance Indicators (KPIs)

Once organizational objectives are established, define specific KPIs that align with these goals. These could include metrics such as conversion rates, customer satisfaction scores, user retention rates, or revenue targets. Ensure that these KPIs are measurable, achievable, and relevant to UX design efforts.

3. Prioritize Goals

Not all business goals are created equal. Prioritize goals based on their strategic importance and potential impact on the organization. Consider factors such as urgency, feasibility, and alignment with long-term objectives when prioritizing goals for UX design initiatives.

4. Communicate and Align

Clearly communicate the identified business goals to all stakeholders involved in the UX design process, including designers, developers, product managers, and executives. Ensure that everyone understands how their work contributes to achieving these goals and aligns with the broader vision of the organization.

By setting clear and measurable business goals for UX design, organizations can ensure that their design efforts are purposeful, impactful, and aligned with broader strategic objectives. With a shared understanding of the desired outcomes, UX professionals can prioritize initiatives, allocate resources effectively, and ultimately drive business success through exceptional user experiences.

CHAPTER THREE
User Research and Analysis

> "
> Design is the bridge between imagination and human interaction.

User research and analysis form the foundation of strategic user experience (UX) design, providing valuable insights into user behaviors, needs, and preferences. In this section, we'll explore the importance of user research and how it informs the design process.

The Importance of User Research

1. Understanding User Needs

User research helps UX designers gain a deep understanding of the target audience's needs, motivations, and pain points. By conducting interviews, surveys, and usability studies, designers can uncover valuable insights that inform design decisions and drive user-centric solutions.

2. Validating Assumptions

User research enables designers to validate their assumptions and hypotheses about user behavior. By testing prototypes and gathering feedback from real users, designers can identify areas for improvement and refine their designs to better meet user needs.

3. Identifying Oppurtunities

Through user research, designers can identify new opportunities for innovation and differentiation. By observing how users interact with existing products or services, designers can uncover unmet needs or pain points that present opportunities for creating unique value propositions.

Methods of User Research

1. Qualitative Research

Qualitative research methods, such as interviews, focus groups, and ethnographic studies, provide in-depth insights into user attitudes, behaviors, and motivations. These methods are particularly useful for understanding the "why" behind user actions and preferences.

2. Quantitative Research

Quantitative research involves gathering numerical data on user behaviour, preferences, and demographics. Methods such as surveys, analytics, and A/B testing can provide valuable statistical insights into user trends and patterns at scale.

3. Contextual Inquiry

Contextual inquiry involves observing users in their natural environment to understand how they interact with products or services in real-world scenarios. By immersing themselves in users' contexts, designers can gain a holistic understanding of their needs and challenges.

Analysis and Synthesis

Once user research data is collected, it's essential to analyze and synthesize the findings to extract meaningful insights. This involves identifying patterns, trends, and themes in the data and distilling them into actionable recommendations for design.

Tools for User Research

Numerous tools and techniques are available to facilitate user research, from online survey platforms and analytics tools to usability testing software and prototyping tools. Choose tools that best suit your research objectives and budget constraints. By conducting thorough user research and analysis, UX designers can gain valuable insights that inform design decisions, validate assumptions, and uncover opportunities for innovation. By integrating user-centric principles into the design process, organizations can create experiences that resonate with users and drive business success.

CHAPTER FOUR

Designing for Target Audience

> “
>
> Crafting tailored experiences for audiences.

Designing for the target audience is a cornerstone of strategic user experience (UX) design, ensuring that products or services resonate with the intended users. Here, we'll explore the importance of understanding the target audience and tailoring design decisions to meet their needs and preferences.

Understanding the Target Audience

1. User Personas

User personas are fictional representations of the target audience based on demographic, psychographic, and behavioral data. Creating user personas helps designers empathize with users and understand their goals, pain points, and motivations.

2. User Journey Mapping

User journey mapping involves visualizing the end-to-end experience of users as they interact with a product or service. By mapping out key touchpoints and emotions along the user journey, designers can identify opportunities to improve the overall user experience.

Tailoring Design Decisions

1. Visual Design

Visual elements such as colors, typography, and imagery play a crucial role in shaping the user experience. Designers should consider the preferences and sensibilities of the target audience when selecting visual elements to ensure that they resonate with users.

2. Information Architecture

Information architecture refers to the organization and structure of content within a product or service. By organizing information in a way that aligns with the mental models of the target audience, designers can make it easier for users to find what they need and navigate the interface seamlessly.

3. Interaction Design

Interaction design focuses on designing intuitive and engaging interactions that guide users through the interface. By understanding the behaviors and expectations of the target audience, designers can create interactions that feel natural and intuitive, enhancing the overall user experience.

Incorporating User Feedback

1. Usability Testing

Usability testing involves observing users as they interact with prototypes or existing products to identify usability issues and gather feedback. By involving users in the design process, designers can validate design decisions and iterate on solutions based on real-world feedback.

2. **Interactive Design**

Iterative design involves continuously refining and improving design solutions based on user feedback and testing results. By adopting an iterative approach, designers can address user needs and preferences iteratively, resulting in a more user-centered and effective design.

Designing for the target audience is essential for creating user experiences that resonate with users and drive business success. By understanding the needs, preferences, and behaviors of the target audience and tailoring design decisions accordingly, designers can create experiences that delight users and achieve organizational goals.

CHAPTER FOUR
Measuring Success Metrics

> “
>
> True success in design is measured by the resonance it creates in users' lives.

Measuring success metrics is a critical aspect of strategic user experience (UX) design, allowing organizations to evaluate the effectiveness of their design efforts and make data-driven decisions. In this section, we'll explore the importance of defining and measuring key performance indicators (KPIs) for UX design initiatives.

Why Measure Success Metrics?

1. Quantify Impact

Success metrics enable organizations to quantify the impact of UX design on key business outcomes, such as user engagement, conversion rates, and revenue generation. By tracking these metrics over time, organizations can assess the effectiveness of their design strategies and identify areas for improvement.

2. Validate Design Decision

Measuring success metrics provides empirical evidence to validate design decisions and hypotheses. By comparing performance of different design iterations or variations through A/B testing or multivariate testing, organizations can identify which design elements are most effective in achieving desired outcomes.

3. Drive Continuous Improvement

Success metrics provide valuable insights for driving continuous improvement in UX design. By identifying trends, patterns, and areas of underperformance, organizations can iterate on design solutions and optimize the user experience over time.

Key Performance Indicators (KPIs) for UX Design

1. Conversion Rates

Conversion rates measure the percentage of users who take a desired action, such as making a purchase, signing up for a newsletter, or completing a form. Tracking conversion rates helps organizations assess the effectiveness of their design in driving user actions and achieving business goals.

2. Rentention Rates

Retention rates measure the percentage of users who continue to engage with a product or service over time. High retention rates indicate that the user experience is compelling and valuable, while low retention rates may signal issues with usability or relevance.

3. User Satisfaction Scores

User satisfaction scores, such as Net Promoter Score (NPS) or Customer Satisfaction Score (CSAT), measure users' overall satisfaction with a product or service. These scores provide valuable

insights into users' perceptions and sentiments, helping organizations identify areas for improvement.

4. **Task Success Rates**

Task success rates measure the percentage of users who successfully complete a specific task or goal within a product or service. By tracking task success rates, organizations can assess the usability and effectiveness of their design in facilitating user tasks and workflows.

Tools for Measuring Success Metrics

Several tools and techniques are available for measuring success metrics in UX design, including analytics platforms, user testing software, and survey tools. Choose tools that align with your measurement objectives and provide actionable insights for optimizing the user experience.

By defining and measuring success metrics for UX design initiatives, organizations can assess the effectiveness of their design strategies, validate design decisions, and drive continuous improvement in the user experience.

CHAPTER FIVE

Implementing Feedback Loops

> “
>
> Feedback loops in UX are the compass guiding continual improvement.

Implementing feedback loops is crucial for ensuring that user experience (UX) design remains aligned with user needs and business goals throughout the product development lifecycle. In this section, we'll explore the importance of feedback loops and strategies for integrating them into the design process.

Why Implement Feedback Loops?

1. **Continuous Improvement**

Feedback loops enable organizations to gather ongoing feedback from users and stakeholders, facilitating continuous improvement in the user experience. By soliciting feedback at various stages of the design process, organizations can identify areas for refinement and optimization.

2. **Validation of Design Decisions**

Feedback loops provide an opportunity to validate design decisions and hypotheses through real-world user feedback. By gathering feedback from users through usability testing, surveys, or user interviews, organizations can assess the effectiveness of their design solutions and make informed decisions.

3. User-Centered Design

Feedback loops promote a user-centered approach to design, ensuring that design decisions are grounded in user needs and preferences. By involving users in the design process and incorporating their feedback, organizations can create experiences that resonate with users and drive engagement.

Strategies for Implementing Feedback Loops

1. Usability Testing

Usability testing involves observing users as they interact with prototypes or existing products to identify usability issues and gather feedback. Conducting regular usability testing sessions throughout the design process allows organizations to validate design decisions and iterate on solutions based on real-world feedback.

2. Surveys and Feedback Forms

Surveys and feedback forms provide a structured way to gather feedback from users on their experiences with a product or service. By soliciting feedback on specific aspects of the user experience, organizations can identify areas for improvement and prioritize design enhancements accordingly.

3. **User Interviews and Focus Groups**

User interviews and focus groups allow organizations to gather qualitative insights into user attitudes, behaviors, and motivations. By conducting in-depth interviews or group discussions, organizations can uncover valuable insights that inform design decisions and drive user-centered solutions.

4. **Feedback Loops in Agile Development**

In agile development environments, feedback loops are integrated into the development process through iterative cycles of design, development, and testing. By soliciting feedback from stakeholders and end users at each iteration, organizations can validate assumptions, address concerns, and adapt their strategies accordingly.

Implementing feedback loops is essential for maintaining a user-centered approach to design and driving continuous improvement in the user experience. By gathering feedback from users and stakeholders throughout the design process, organizations can validate design decisions, identify areas for improvement, and create experiences that resonate with users and drive business success.

CONCLUSION

> "
>
> In UX, the conclusion is where users find satisfaction and fulfillment.

In the fast-paced world of digital product development, strategic user experience (UX) design is more critical than ever. Throughout this eBook, we've explored the fundamental principles and strategies for aligning user needs with business goals to create exceptional user experiences that drive success.

From setting clear business goals and conducting user research to designing for the target audience and measuring success metrics, every step of the UX design process plays a crucial role in delivering value to both users and organizations. By integrating user-centric principles into the design process and continuously iterating based on feedback, organizations can create experiences that resonate with users and achieve meaningful business outcomes.

As you embark on your journey to enhance UX design within your organization, remember the following key takeaways:

1. **Alignment with Business Goals**

Ensure that UX design efforts are aligned with broader organizational objectives, focusing on initiatives that drive tangible value and contribute to business success.

2. **User-Centric Approach**

Put users at the center of the design process, empathizing with their needs, preferences, and behaviors to create experiences that are intuitive, engaging, and meaningful.

3. **Continuous Improvement**

Embrace a culture of continuous improvement, leveraging feedback loops and iterative design processes to refine and optimize the user experience over time.

4. **Data-Driven Decisions**

Make informed decisions based on data and insights gathered through user research, usability testing, and performance metrics, prioritizing initiatives that have the greatest impact on user satisfaction and business outcomes.

By adopting these principles and strategies, organizations can unlock the full potential of strategic UX design to drive user engagement, foster customer loyalty, and differentiate their products or services in a competitive marketplace.

Notice of Copyright

Edited By:

Dhayanandh Ravichandran

First Printing Edition, 2024

ISBN 978-93-340-1938-4

www.ingramcontent.com/pod-product-compliance
Lightning Source LLC
LaVergne TN
LVHW021356160826
845679LV00008B/1639

* 9 7 8 9 3 3 4 0 1 9 3 8 4 *